LONDON
GRAFFITI

LONDON GRAFFITI

PHOTOGRAPHED BY JAC CHAROUX

Introduction by
JOHN COOPER CLARKE

W.H. ALLEN. London
A Howard & Wyndham Company
1980

Printed and bound in Great Britain by
Waterlow (Dunstable) Ltd.
for the Publishers, W.H. Allen & Co. Ltd,
44 Hill Street, London W1X 8LB

ISBN 0 491 02813 X

CITY OF LONDON
LONDON WALL
E.C.2.
PAPER
City Recorder
CENTRAL LONDON'S LOCAL NEWSPAPER
CALL FOR WALKWAY ALONG ROMAN WALL
ALDERSGATE ELECTION:
McWILLIAMS 291
SILK 279
THURSDAYS
8p

CADILLACS
ONLY

INTRODUCTION

Many years ago, whilst making use of a public convenience, I was introduced to the world of Mr Kilroy, legendary poet of the pissoir. There, among inaccurate depictions of the female form and the telephone numbers of various perverts, could be found his scatological musings:

'You don't come here to piss about
So have a piss and piss off out.'

I was reminded of my own importance in the evolutionary process of mankind by the phrase: Gentlemen, the future of Britain is in your hands. These and many more such items are indellibly scrawled on the tiles of my subconscious. They were my first encounter with that age old phenomenon, graffiti.

The invention of the aerosol paint spray expanded the graffiti artists' realm of operation, enabling them to use brighter and more imaginative colour schemes. Urban renewal presented larger and flatter surfaces, effectively taking the word out of the closet and onto the streets; flyovers, subways, municipal facilities and housing estates seem incomplete without the names of football teams, pop stars, youth cults, lovers and someone you've never heard of who rules OK!

Popular Art Form or Visual Pollutant? The question is irrelevant. Graffiti, particularly the sprayed variety, is an aspect of modern iconography which has been seized upon by the communication-conscious world of pop music and those unpaid agents of publicity: the fans. Given that graffiti is an extra-legal pursuit, any new pop group would be well advised to choose a short name, enabling their fans to spray and scarper in the shortest possible time. I suspect that this is one reason why my own combo 'The Invisible Girls' are not so familiar as 999 or Led Zep. The laws of brevity, however, do not always dictate the content of these spraycan manifestoes. I have seen 100 yards of William Blake carefully committed, in florid script, to a sizeable stretch of wall in West London. Concrete Poetry, I should koko.

Most graffiti does not betray such delicate sensibilities, rather it remains the only existing platform for the socio/political malcontent, the inarticulate outsider of the sub-literate character assassin. Like vandalism, Kung Fu or action painting, graffiti is a minority pursuit. *You* don't write on walls, *I* don't write on walls but we are all, at some time or other, intrigued by the products of those who do. None of us escape such unanswerable questions as: 'Who put the cunt in Scunthorpe?'

In the year eighteen-twenty-something when Victor Hugo was exploring Notre Dame cathedral he found, carved by hand on the wall, in the dark recess of one of the towers, the word: ΑΝΑΓΚΗ These capitals, blackened with age, cut deep in the stone, conveyed a grim and fatal import which made a keen impression of the author. Since then the wall has been distempered or scraped or both and the inscription has gone. There is nothing left of the unknown destiny of which it was so cheerless a summary.

In eighteen-thirty-one Victor Hugo commenced work on *The Hunchback of Notre Dame,* the book that made him famous. ΑΝΑΓΚΗ is a Greek word. It means 'Fatality'.
The aforementioned book was written about that word. Still on the subject of great writers, some of my own work, for example, 'Psycle Sluts' was originally inspired by such anonymous verbiage.

I feel sorry for people who are disgusted by graffiti, since we are surrounded by it. This book highlights the picturesque aspects of such familiar visual phenomena.

Kilroy is here to stay.

MORE PLEASE

A public expression of pent-up aggression in Notting Hill Gate

Police graffiti? Great Western Road, W9

ABOVE: *No comment!*

OPPOSITE: *So right for it's environment — a street inhabited by squatters in Streatham*

NOTHING
LASTS

Poem written on the ground of a roller skating area in Latimer Road, W10

SOFT & SMOOTH

One of my favourites — in Holland Park, where many artists live

This was possibly written by a frustrated artist outside the AIR Gallery in Shaftesbury Avenue, which has now been pulled down

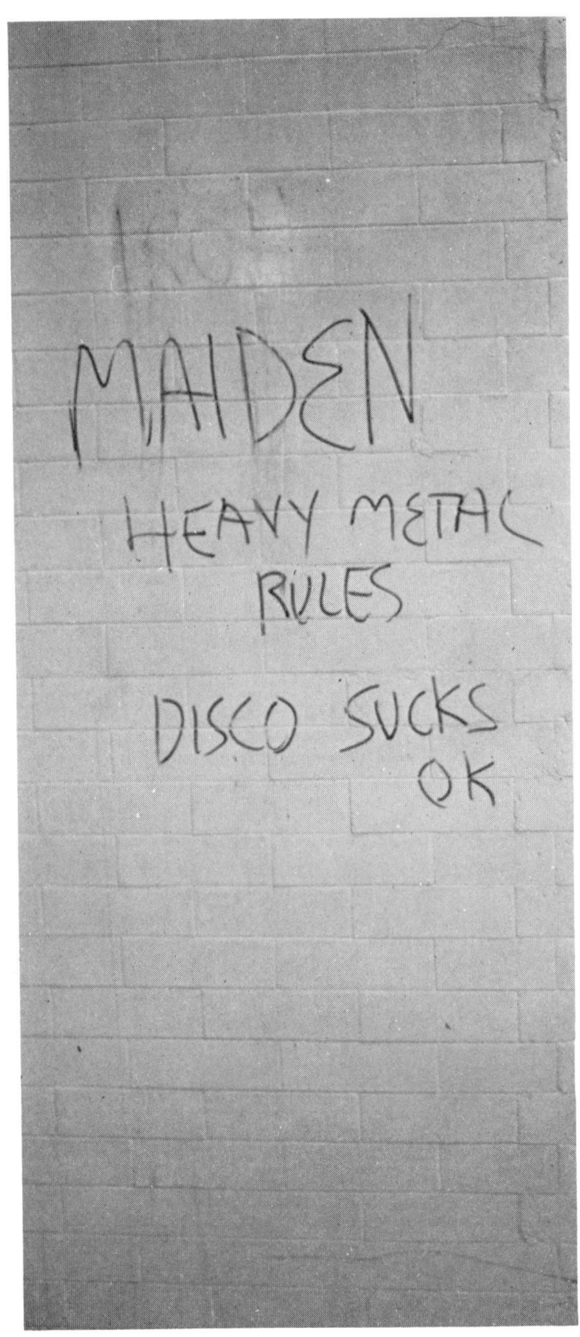
MAIDEN
HEAVY METAL
RULES
DISCO SUCKS
OK

. . . *pay later?*

Portobello Road, W11

Black consciousness on Ladbroke Grove tube station

Recipe for a sleepless night?

Although not strictly graffiti, this was an amusing back-street surprise

Mural and messages from squatters in Streatham

LAMBETH
COUNCIL
SOCIAL SECURITY HOSTEL

DEATH
TO
DISCO!

A left-over from the drug era of five years ago

O.K!

Line by Bob Dylan used humorously as an anti-establishment slogan in Notting Hill Gate

This one in Fulham dates back to Jubilee year 1977

How sweet! Portobello Road, W11

He would probably be on strike by now!

Not a soul was dangling around!

ALL THE WORLD'S AN OPIUM DEN
AND ALL the PLAYERS merely ADDICTS

ALL THE WORLD'S AN OPIUM DEN
AND ALL the PLAYERS merely ADDICTS
THROBBING GRISTLE

Cynical comment which appeared recently in Porchester Road, Paddington

ROCK
AGAINST
THATCHER

Streatham hedonist

I thought they ate out of newspaper — but it had to be The Guardian *or* The Times!

Based on the famous advertisement for Smirnoff vodka. Great Western Road, W9

Would we dare!

The only one I saw being written — by a teenage couple. She wrote it, and he added 'pussy'

A Cockney relic dating from Jubilee year

The woman in this picture looks as confused as I am by this message

FIGHT FOR THE RIGHT TO WORK

Ladbroke Grove anti-nuclear statement

A very witty anti-nuclear statement

Comment on the Housing Trust. And the suggestion for how to use one's birth certificate (in Notting Hill Gate) has now disappeared

The lady walking by seemed to confirm the truth behind these words in St James' Garden, Holland Park

Near Chelsea College of Art in the King's Road

Obedience is suicide

NF
NO
MAKE
LOUSY
LOVERS

One of the many pieces of graffiti which decorate pillars under the Westway flyover between Ladbroke Grove and Portobello Road

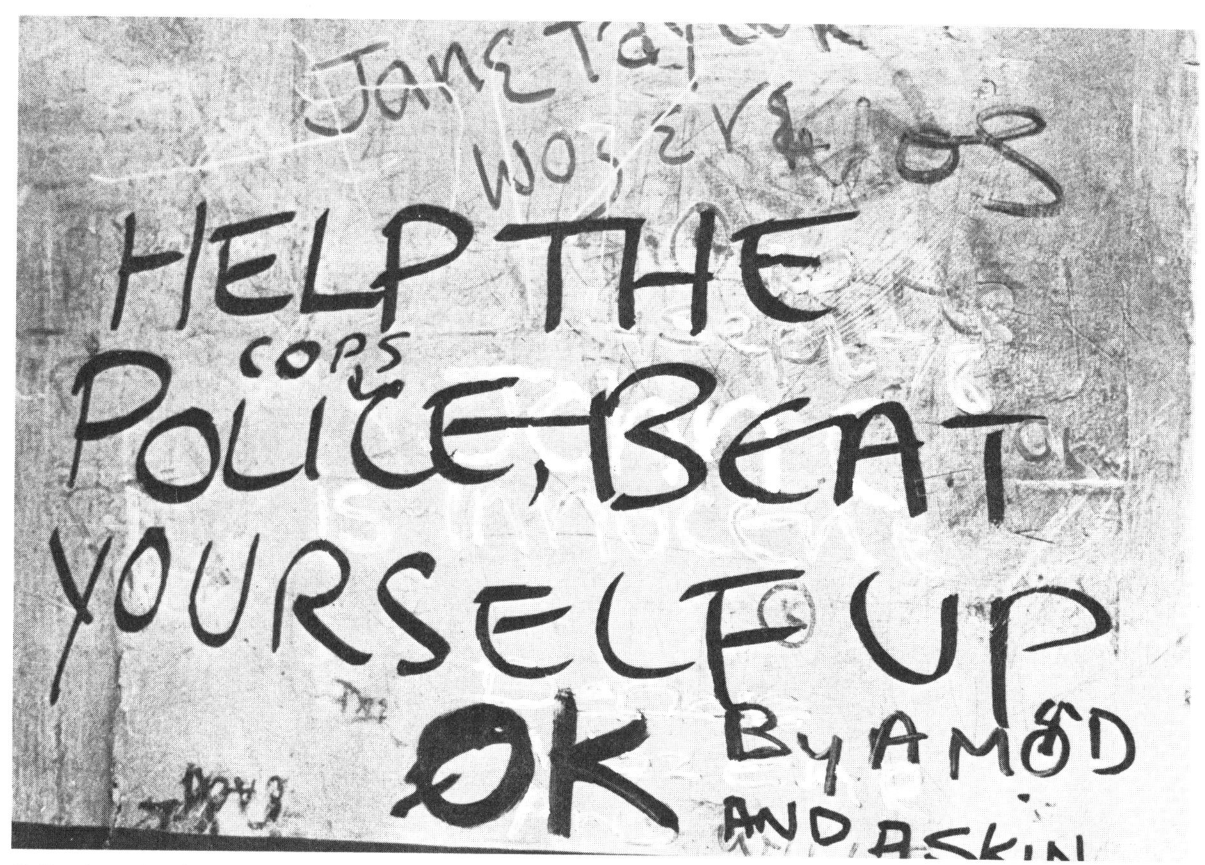

Police brutality has reached the headlines in Upper Street, Islington

. . . says Camden Lock's wise man

A familiar slogan in Notting Hill Gate

Why put
a roun

well
us?

ABOVE: *So is graffiti!*

OPPOSITE: *This was written a few years ago in Covent Garden Market, but has now disappeared*

fighting for
peace
is like
fucking
for virginity

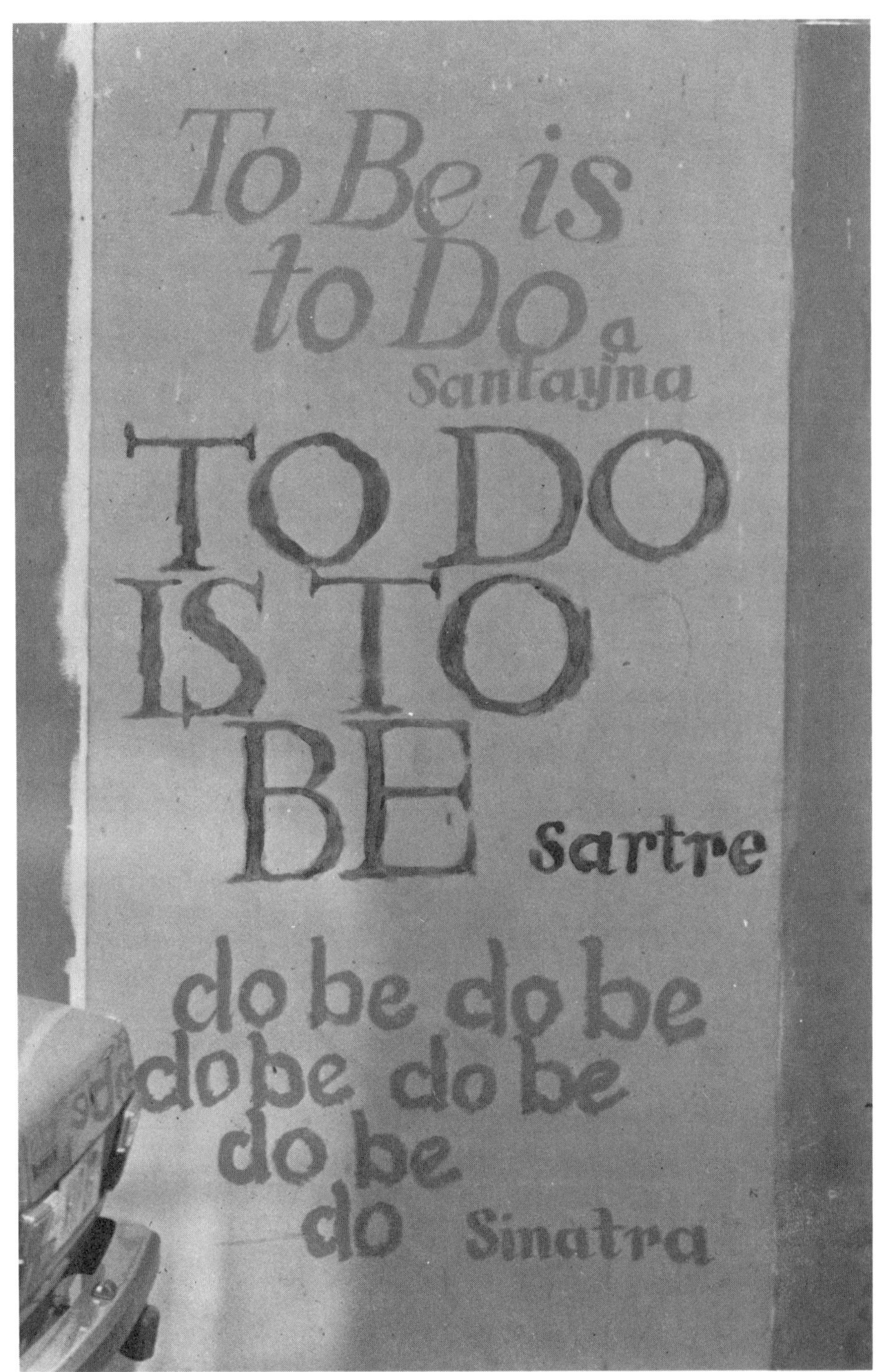

One which is a favourite in men's toilets, this time written on boards in Covent Garden

Wise words south of the river

Another rock group?

Now we know where Guinness got the idea!

Don't we roll anymore?

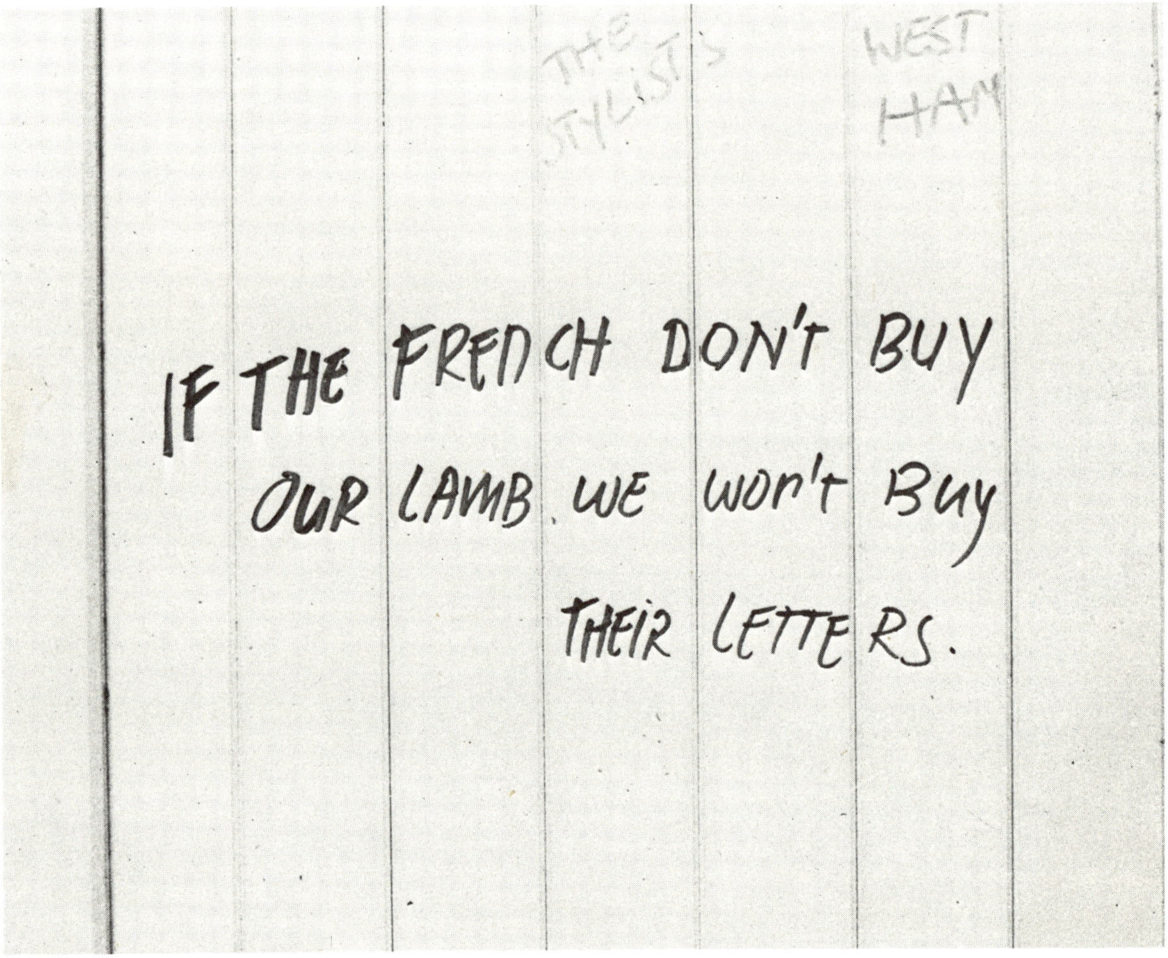

Trade warfare — a last resort?

That magic word

One of the very few pieces of graffiti written on the pavement — this one is in Holland Park

A rare pro-nuclear comment in Courtfield Road, South Kensington

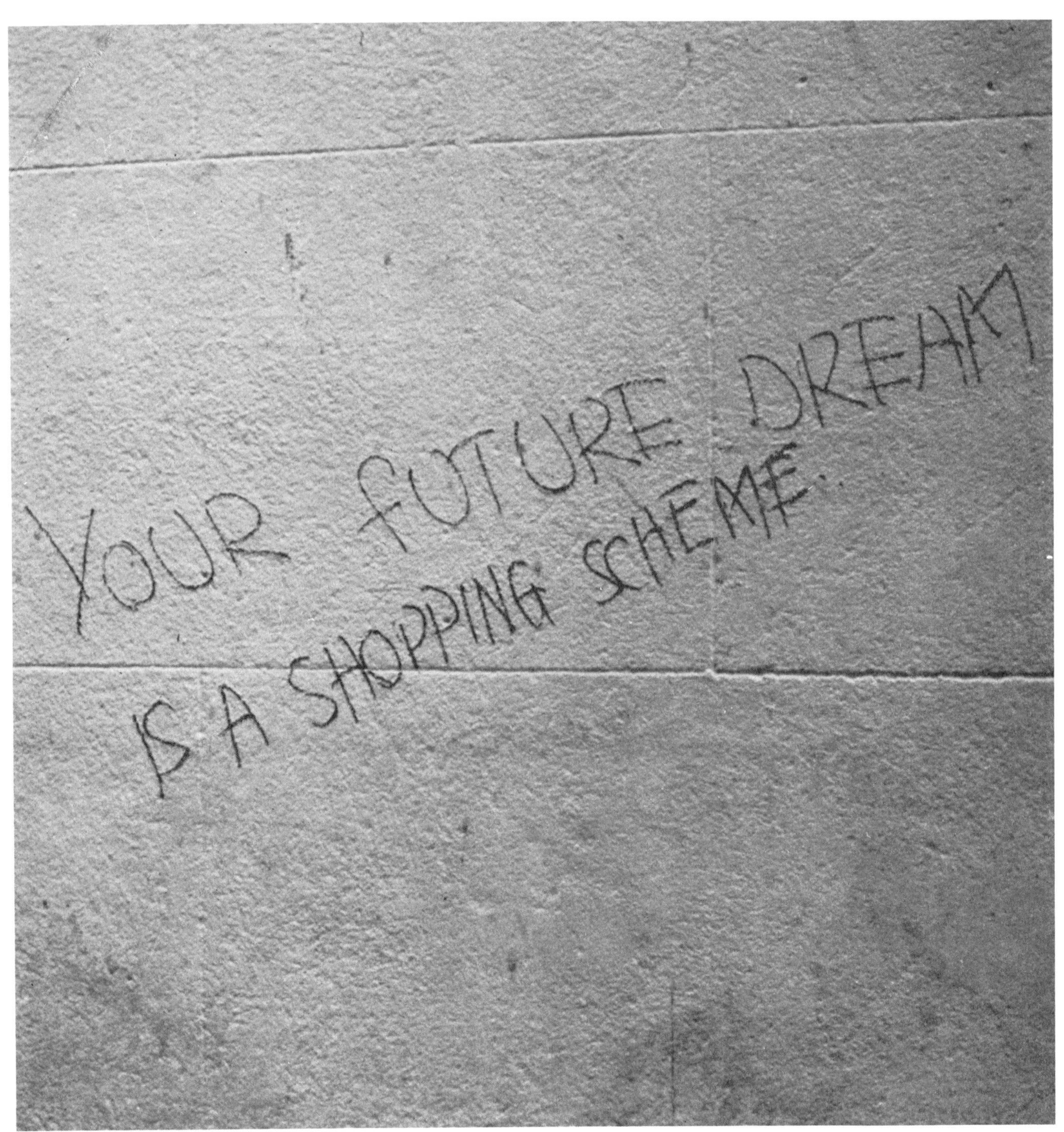

Sarcastic comment about Covent Garden's new development

Obscurity is the message . . .

ABOVE: *On a bridge in Priory Road, NW6. This graffiti (top) has been here for years but the new twist (bottom) was added recently*

OPPOSITE: *Unexpected place for this comment in Charing Cross*

SORE ARSE

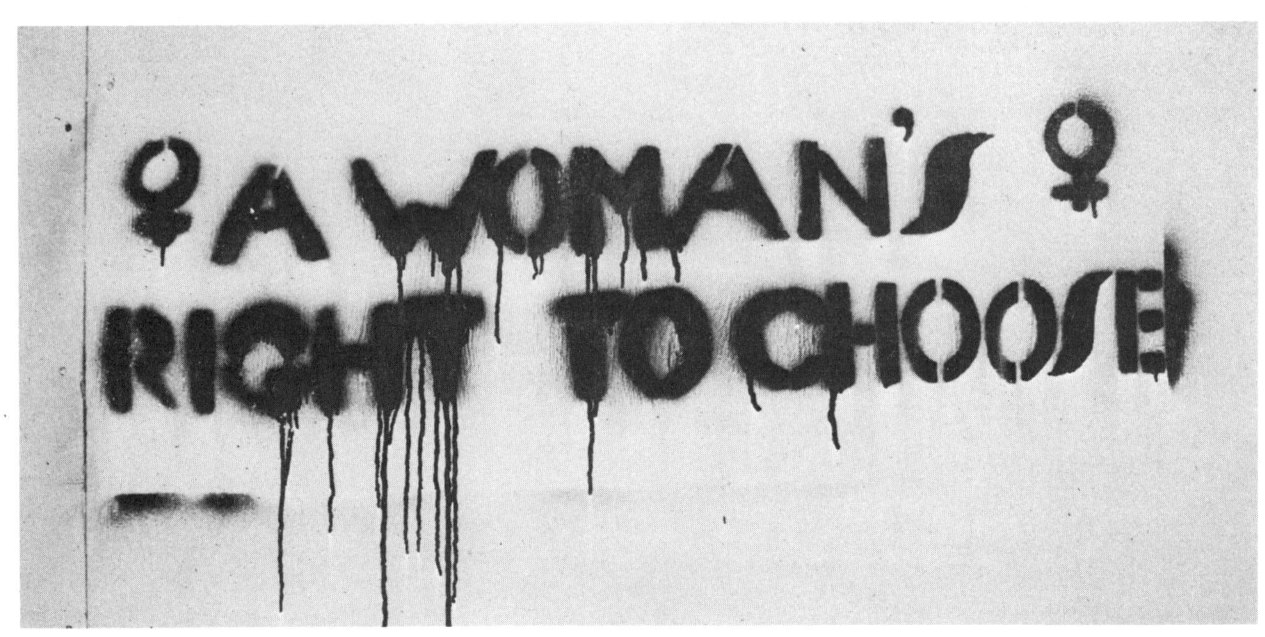

A recent pro-abortion slogan in Fulham

An early piece of feminist graffiti, photographed five years ago in Notting Hill Gate

I think this photograph speaks for itself

U.F.O.
LIVES

King's Road aspirations, but this message is no longer there

Is that all?

Two wise words from the birds in Island *by Aldous Huxley, tied together with Sansckrit*

I FOUGHT THE LAW
OSSINGTON
STREET W2
CITY OF WESTMINSTER

RAZORS PAIN YOU.
RIVERS ARE DAMP.
ACIDS STAIN YOU.
DRUGS CAUSE CRAMP
GUNS AREN'T LAWFUL
NOOSES GIVE.
GAS SMELLS AWFUL.
YOU MIGHT AS WELL LIVE...

ABOVE: *Thought-provoking question on a wall in Notting Hill Gate*

OPPOSITE: *Blandford Street, W1*

He obviously doesn't believe in the 16th century French poet's predictions!

By the side of a pub in Holland Park. It started as Art, changed to Tart and ended up in its present state!

A surrealist touch in Notting Hill Gate

left hand drive

Businessman's approach to the shortage of accommodation in London

Appropriately written in Wimbledon

Those who lead the world
into the abyss call ruling
too difficult for US!

WE ARE ALL
MONGOLOÏDS
DEVO

The most recent comment I have seen from the anti-nuclear movement

Wishful thinking

From an élitist consumer in Streatham!

Written on a boarded-up house in a derelict area

Another take-off of the Smirnoff advertisement — this time in Kilburn

Probably the same 'author' who wrote the Smirnoff take-off, this graffiti uses the cliché of the equally famous Heineken advertisement

More cynicism directed at our leaders

Really? This is certainly news to me

Gloucester Road, Kensington—this is one of the last pieces of graffiti, I found